Dr Anne Townsend

Marvellous Me

Illustrations by Saroj Vaghela

A LION BOOK

Copyright © 1984 Lion Publishing

Published by
Lion Publishing plc
Icknield Way, Tring, Herts, England
ISBN 0 85648 577 2
Albatross Books
PO Box 320, Sutherland, NSW 2232, Australia
ISBN 0 86760 499 9

First edition 1984

Photographs by Alan Hutchison Library 2 (left hand page, below),
Lion Publishing/Jon Willcocks 16, Picturepoint 2 (right hand page,
both), 3, 10, 14, 15, 19 (right hand page), Spectrum Colour Library
6, 20 (right hand page), ZEFA cover and title page, 1, 2 (left
hand page, above), 5, 7, 11, 12 (both), 13, 19 (left hand page)

Printed in Portugal
by Printer Portuguesa Industria Grafica LDA

CONTENTS

It's amazing!

The way the human body works is amazing. It's so intricate and complicated, it makes you ask lots of questions.

Why does my heart beat fast when I run?

Why do I get out of breath?

What happens if you break your neck?

What does my brain do?

What happens to the food we eat?

How do muscles work?
Why do people have different coloured skins?
Why do sweet and sour taste different?
How does bleeding stop?
How does a baby start to grow inside its mother?

I am 'me' and you are 'you'

Do you know anyone who looks exactly like you? Unless you are an identical twin, you won't find anyone in the whole world who looks exactly like you.

You are special because you are different from anybody else. Your family think you are important because they love you. But have you ever stopped to think that God made you just as you are because he loves you and wanted there to be a *you* in the world?

Look closely at your index finger (that's the finger nearest your thumb). Look at it through a magnifying glass. On the pad of that finger you can see tiny grooves and ridges in a pattern. No two people in the whole world have the same fingerprints.

It's easy to see the outside of a person's body — arms, legs, face, feet and hands. But inside a person, under the skin, is a miraculous inner world that never stops working until you die. Inside are the big organs like your lungs and your heart. And there are nerves and blood vessels, muscles and bones, which connect everything together.

Your body cannot work unless all the different parts work together, and each part does what it's supposed to do — in the right way and at the right time.

God's design for the human body is amazing and wonderful.

If you press your finger on an ink-pad and then on to paper, you have made your own fingerprint.

Twenty-four hour pump—the heart

Why does my heart beat fast when I run?

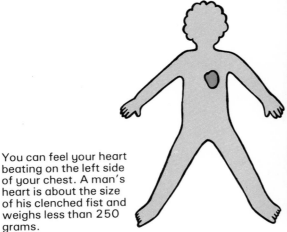

You can feel your heart beating on the left side of your chest. A man's heart is about the size of his clenched fist and weighs less than 250 grams.

The heart pumps blood round the body. The blood has to supply energy to all parts of the body. When you run, your leg muscles need extra energy, so your heart beats faster.

Although the heart isn't very big, it is very important. It has to keep beating all day, every day. If it stops beating for more than three minutes, you'll probably die — unless you are kept alive on an artificial heart and lung machine.

The heart works like a pump. It is very efficient. With every beat it pumps one cup of blood through your blood vessels. There are valves inside your heart to stop the blood running back, to make sure it goes in the right direction.

In one minute your heart can pump seven litres of blood round your body. When you are running or exercising hard, it can pump as much as fourteen litres round the body in one minute to get energy to all the parts of the body.

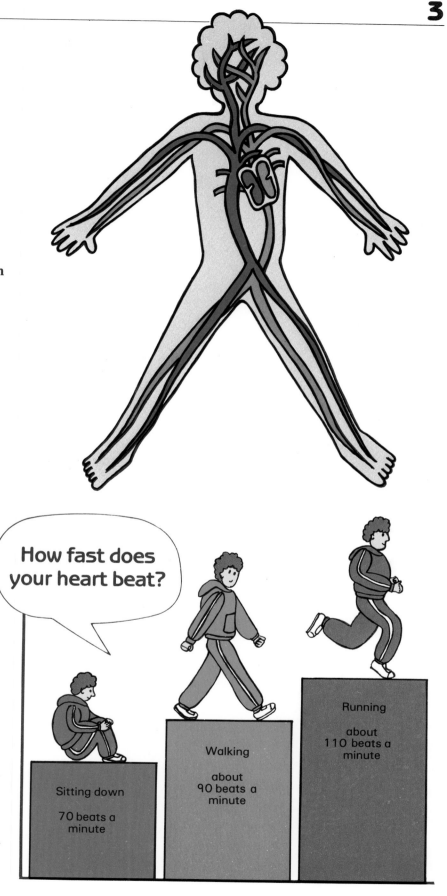

> **When the heart beats where does the blood go?**

The blood travels in tubes called arteries to get to the different parts of the body. It travels back to the heart in tubes called veins.

This network of tubes is rather like a tree. The veins and arteries are branches. Near the surface of the skin are lots of tiny tubes, like twigs, called blood vessels.

In arteries the blood is bright red because it has come from the lungs full of oxygen. The blood has to supply lots of good things, including energy and oxygen, to all parts of the body.

The blood in the veins is purplish-red because it carries only a small amount of oxygen. The veins carry the 'used' blood back to the heart and lungs to get it 'cleaned' and full of oxygen again. In veins there are valves to stop the blood running back. The valves in your legs are very strong.

When the heart has pumped the used blood through to the lungs and it is bright red and full of oxygen again, then it goes back to the heart to be sent off around the body through the arteries once more.

This process — the circulatory system — never stops throughout your life. And the heart is the centre of it all.

> **How fast does your heart beat?**

Sitting down
70 beats a minute

Walking
about
90 beats a minute

Running
about
110 beats a minute

What is blood?

The blood pumping round your body is a busy transport system carrying a lot of traffic. It is made of a red liquid that carries oxygen, energy, food, messengers and waste products from one part of the body to another very quickly.

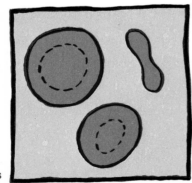

red blood cells

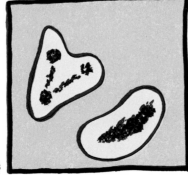

white blood cells

If you look at your blood under a microscope, you will see that it is made up of a yellow-ish fluid, called plasma. The fluid is teeming with clumps of red blood cells that look like miniature flying saucers. Dotted in between these are different white blood cells. You can't see the oxygen, waste products or special messengers that whizz around your body in the blood fluid.

The chemical messengers, called hormones, travel at high speed from one part to the other, telling your body what to do and what not to do. They help to make sure that each part of your body works in harmony with other parts. They control the speed at which you grow, so that it's not too fast and not too slow. They make sure that if you are a boy you look like a boy, and if you are a girl you look like a girl. And they also make sure that your food is used properly.

What do blood cells do?

The red blood cells grab hold of oxygen and broken-down food, and rush it to the parts of your body that need it. That is how each part of you has the energy it needs to do its work. God has made everything so that every part works together to make sure you always have enough energy in vital parts like your brain and heart — the parts that never stop working.

Your white blood cells are important in battling against germs. Sometimes they massacre germs and carry them out of harm's way. At other times they shoot off anti-bodies which paralyse or kill the germs.

How does bleeding stop?

When your nose bleeds or you cut yourself, the bleeding usually stops without anyone doing anything. If you cut a vein or an artery then it is more difficult to get the bleeding to stop.

If you cut yourself, the tiny blood vessels in the skin close up as soon as they have been damaged. Then special agents in the blood, called clotting factors, do their work. They come from the plasma and from the red blood cells. When they are all blended together they form a tough clot that stops blood from getting out and germs from getting in. A scab is a dried-out blood clot. If you pick a scab then you dislodge everything and the bleeding starts again.

Spring cleaners—lungs

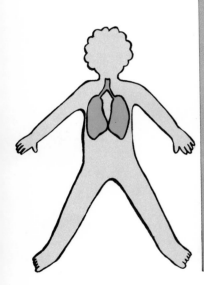

What are lungs?
Where are they?

You have two lungs, one on each side of your chest. When you breathe, you can feel your chest going in and out. Your lungs are like two trees, with twigs at the very end. At the tips of the tiny lung tubes are tiny balloons. These fill with air and it is here that oxygen gets into the blood, and waste carbon dioxide is washed out into the air you breathe out.

You never really stop breathing until you die because your lungs supply your blood with oxygen — and oxygen is vital for life.

As soon as a baby is born it yells and then starts to breathe for the first time, taking fresh air down the windpipe to the lungs.

In your lungs your blood is 'cleaned' — all waste gases are washed out; and fresh oxygen is put in.

Why do I get out of breath?

When you exercise, your body needs extra oxygen.

So, your heart beats fast to get blood round your body as quickly as possible. And you have to breathe fast to supply your blood with extra oxygen, and to wash out the carbon dioxide that is made during exercise.

When you breathe in your lungs get bigger, and when you breathe out they get smaller as all the air is pushed out.

Breathe in deeply and measure round your chest. Then breathe out, and measure it again. If you are very healthy there will be 3 to 5 centimetres difference between the two measurements.

What is a yawn?

When you yawn you are usually feeling tired or sleepy.

You yawn because — without you knowing it — your brain tells your lungs to help you wake up. You breathe very deeply without thinking about it first. This pulls extra air into your lungs to freshen them and help you wake up.

What is a hiccup?

You can stop hiccups by getting a cup full of water and then drinking from it by bending over the cup and sipping the water from the wrong side of the cup.

When you hiccup you breathe in and out sharply and quickly. After each breath your voice-box closes with a snap and that makes you go 'hic'.

There are lots of different reasons why you hiccup. If you can't stop hiccuping for several days then it might mean that you are ill — otherwise it doesn't matter.

Food processing—stomach and intestines

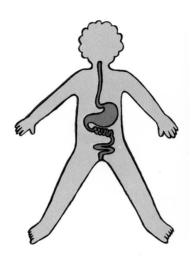

What happens to the food we eat?

The body must have food to supply it with energy. Energy is needed for all the different things the body does.

But food doesn't get straight from your mouth to the places where the energy is needed. Your body works hard on your food to break it down and make it useful. The body needs other things from food, too — different sorts of food to help you grow and keep you healthy. You can read about food in part 7.

When you have chewed all your food and swallowed it, it goes down a tube straight into your stomach. This is only the start of a long journey through the body which takes about 24 to 30 hours, by which time all the goodness has been taken out of the food.

Your food stays in your stomach for about an hour. Here it is softened up by special chemicals. When it is nice and liquid, a valve at the end of your stomach opens and the food is pushed down into the first part of your intestines.

Food doesn't usually move backwards as there are valves to stop this. But if you are sick and you vomit, it is because there is something wrong and your stomach squeezes backwards, propelling half-digested food back into your mouth.

In your intestines a complicated and marvellous process goes on for about 30 hours to break down your food so that it is ready to be carried off all over the body. At least 17 different chemicals are used in the intestines to help get each kind of food ready for your body to use.

When your body has extracted all the goodness it needs out of your food, the waste food goes on travelling right down to the very end of your intestines. It comes out of the body when you go to the lavatory.

Some foods do not need much work to break them down; others need a lot. A glucose drink contains sugar in a form your body can use quickly without having to do much to it. So, when you drink a glucose drink you will probably find that you quickly have a burst of energy.

But when you eat a hamburger and chips you won't feel full of energy because your stomach and intestines have a lot of hard work to change that food into a substance that can be carried in the blood all over the body.

Food, glorious food

Why do we need to eat?

You have already seen that your body needs food to change it into energy. You need energy to live, so that your body can work properly, and so that you can run, jump, hop, skip and cycle.

You also need food to help you grow and to keep your body in good repair.

Eating food is fun. You'd probably like to have your favourite food at every meal. But after a time that would make you ill because you need a balance of the right foods to keep you fit. You would certainly get tired of your favourite food but, more important, your body would get weak.

Food makes you grow. The blood carries digested foodstuffs round your body to where it is needed.

Protein is the most important food for building up your body. If you have too much sugar then instead of building up your body, you get fat.

What sort of food helps you to grow?

To be really fit, you need a balance of food containing different kinds of food — we call them proteins, fats, vegetables, carbohydrates and fibre.

Protein—for growth and repair
fish, eggs, meat, milk, cheese, cereals, nuts, beans, lentils, peas

Fats—for fuel
Butter, margarine, oils

Carbohydrates—for energy
sugar, potatoes, bread, cereals, root vegetables, biscuits, cakes

Fibre—found in some vegetables and in whole-grain foods

As well as a good diet you need to make sure that your food contains vitamins. Your body cannot store vitamins and it can't manufacture most of them, and so you must be sure you eat food containing them.

When vitamins were first discovered they were called after letters of the alphabet. New vitamins are still being discovered by scientists.

Vitamins

A—found in dairy products, eggs, fruit, vegetables

B—found in eggs, meat, wholewheat, oats, yeast

C—found in fruit—especially oranges

D—found in eggs, butter, margarine, oily fish

Why do people get thin if they don't eat?

Your body stores any food that it doesn't need to use straight away, ready for when it might need it. Different kinds of food are stored in different places. Some food is stored in the fat parts of your body.

Everyone is different. You can eat the same amount of food as your friend, and he gets fat but you don't. Your body needs energy, even if you are doing nothing — your heart is always beating, your blood is circulating and your lungs are working. All these things happen without you thinking about it. This means that you are using energy all the time.

Energy is measured in calories. If you stop eating then you have to get calories from somewhere. So, your body uses food that is stored as fat. If you try to slim too hard then you can make yourself ill because your body takes energy from places where it should not.

How can I stay healthy?

God has given you a wonderful body to live in. He loves the 'you' he has put in the world. That's why he intends you to look after your body carefully by eating the right sort of food, getting enough sleep and having enough exercise to stay fit.

The body's waste disposal units—kidneys

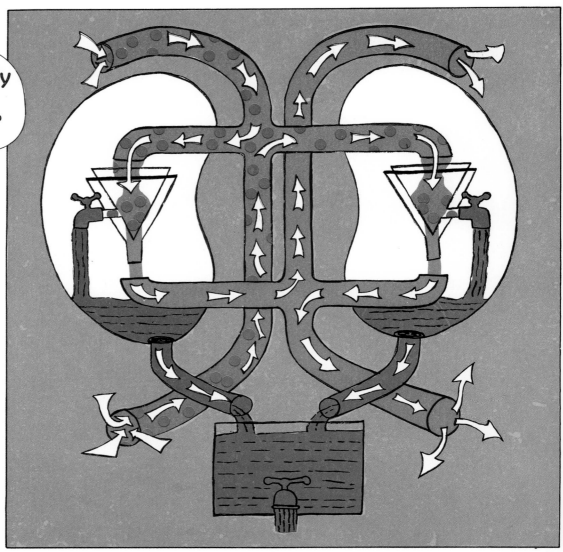

The blood is an excellent transport system. As well as taking good things round the body, it also carries away waste products.

As your cells and tissues work, they make waste stuff which must be removed or you will die. Your blood carries carbon dioxide away to the lungs and other waste to your kidneys.

Each time your heart beats it pumps blood round your body. One-fifth of it goes to be filtered through your kidneys and comes out clean. Meanwhile the waste products travel out from each kidney as urine. This passes down a tube to your bladder at the bottom of your tummy. Your bladder has a strong valve in it. This stops your urine from leaking out all the time. When you go to the lavatory, the valve relaxes and opens so that urine is allowed out.

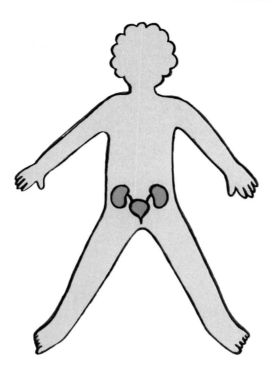

You have two kidneys lying at the back of you just below the bottom of your chest. Each is quite small — about 10 centimetres long, and weighing about 150 grams.

What is a kidney transplant?

Kidneys are capable of doing far more work than they usually do. This means that you can stay fit and alive with only one kidney.

But, if someone's kidneys have stopped working he can only stay alive by using an artificial kidney — a machine which filters his blood to remove the waste — or by being given someone else's kidney.

Nowadays surgeons are able to find out whether or not a certain kidney is suitable for a patient whose kidneys have stopped working. If it is suitable, then they are able to take a kidney from one person and stitch it into place in the person who would otherwise die. Surgeons know how to attach everything so perfectly that the transplanted kidney works, giving new life to the patient.

The body's building blocks—cells

> How are all the different parts of my body put together?

In the same way that your house is built of thousands of bricks, so your body is built out of millions of cells.

There are so many cells that it would be impossible for anyone to try to count them. They are so small that you can't see them without a microscope.

All cells are made in the same basic pattern. But God has designed different cells in different shapes to work in different parts of the body.

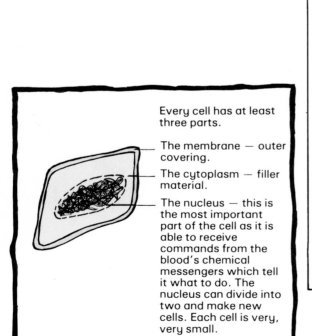

Every cell has at least three parts.

The membrane — outer covering.

The cytoplasm — filler material.

The nucleus — this is the most important part of the cell as it is able to receive commands from the blood's chemical messengers which tell it what to do. The nucleus can divide into two and make new cells. Each cell is very, very small.

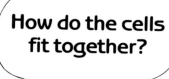

What do different cells look like?

There are different cells in different parts of your body. Here are some of them magnified many times.

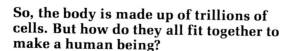

How do the cells fit together?

So, the body is made up of trillions of cells. But how do they all fit together to make a human being?

Groups of cells make up tissues. All muscle cells make up muscle tissue. All bone cells make up bone tissue.

Tissues get together to make organs — like the heart and the lungs. Each organ is made up of tissues to make it work properly. The organs work together to make the body function properly.

Cells are the basic building blocks used to make human beings. You cannot have people without cells.

Did you know that a person starts life as two cells joining together? A cell from the mother and a cell from the father join together and they start to grow into a human being.

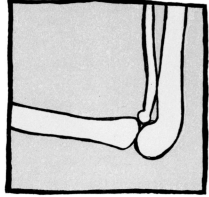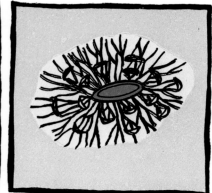

Bone cells

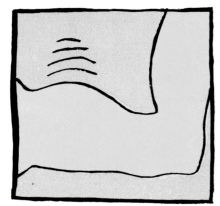

Muscle cells

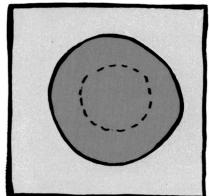

Blood cells

30 000 000 000 000 000 000

Your brain contains billions of cells. There are about 30 trillion red blood cells in an adult human being. Other parts of the body are made up of billions of cells.

How a baby is made

How does a baby start to grow inside its mother?

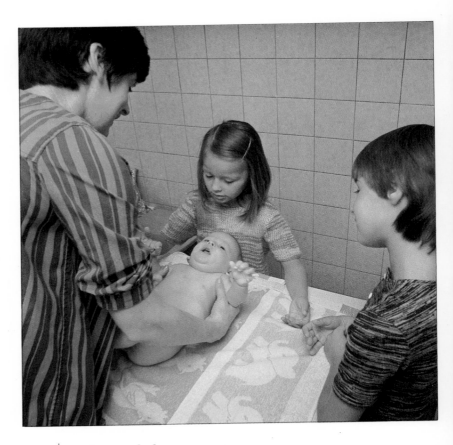

It is obvious that boys' and girls' bodies look different — a boy has a penis, but a girl doesn't. And when they grow up, there is a more obvious difference — a woman can have a baby, but a man cannot.

God designed men and women to be different. He made them to be partners — male and female, mother and father. God made them like this, so that their difference would allow them to say 'I love you!' in a special way. What's more, he created people so that when they love their partner in this way they sometimes have a baby. And that's a very miraculous kind of loving.

But if you have a baby, you are responsible for looking after your baby. And that is why a child's body isn't developed enough to grow a baby. As a child grows up and becomes a teenager, changes take place — a boy begins to produce sperms, and a girl starts to produce eggs from her ovaries every month and has a monthly 'period'. A young teenager is usually developed enough to have a baby — but doesn't want to yet because there's a lot of growing up still to do.

God made babies as helpless creatures who are not able to look after themselves for many years. That is why babies need grown-ups. Babies need a mother and a father to help them grow up — although you can grow up all right with just one of your parents or with other people taking the place of parents if necessary.

When a husband is with his wife, sometimes he feels he loves her very much. His penis knows how he is feeling and it fills up with blood so that it gets stiff. When the wife cuddles her husband close and feels how much she loves him, then an opening between her legs — called the vagina — gets warm and slippery. The man then gently pushes his penis into the woman's vagina. It feels good and loving to both of them. The man then fountains a shower of tiny sperms in fluid into the woman's vagina. And that feels extra good!

The sperms swim like tadpoles up through the woman's vagina into her womb — the special place where a baby grows. As the sperms dance upwards and meet an ovum (egg), then one sperm will join with it. This then starts to grow into a baby.

If no sperms reach the woman's egg, the lining of the womb slips off each month and she bleeds a little. This is called having a monthly 'period'.

Having a baby is one of the most exciting gifts God gives to a family.

All human beings have the same sort of cells to make up their bodies. But men have a special kind of cell that women do not have — sperms. And women have special cells that men do not have — ova or eggs. The cells are very, very small.

A marvellous thing happens when a sperm joins to an ovum. When these two cells meet and join they contain everything necessary to make a completely new person. When the cells unite a tiny baby usually begins to grow.

The birth of a baby

How do two cells turn into a baby?

When the male sperm cell and female egg cell meet then something quite amazing happens. God has made sure that there are instructions in the nucleus of the sperm and of the egg (ovum) explaining exactly what sort of person that baby is to grow into.

Sometimes people say to you, 'You look just like your father,' or 'Those two sisters look alike.' This is because a 'family likeness' is passed down through generations — from even further back than parents, grandparents and great-grandparents. In some families all the members are tall, in others they all have big noses. These things run in families. You are what you are, partly because of what has been passed on to you.

But God made sure that each person is exactly the kind of person that he planned he, or she, should be. Scientists now understand a lot about how a baby grows so we know more and more about the wonderful way a baby is made. God made *you* like *you* because he wanted the world to have you in it.

Passing on the family likeness.

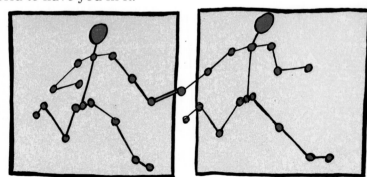

How does a baby grow? How long does it take?

As soon as the sperm and ovum join together they begin to divide into two and then into four, and so on rapidly, until there are lots of cells.

It takes 38 weeks, or just over 9 months, for a baby to develop in its mother before it is really ready to be born.

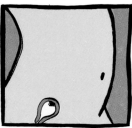

When a sperm joins to an ovum a tiny baby begins to grow.

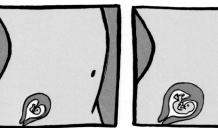

After eight weeks the developing baby begins to look like a human being.

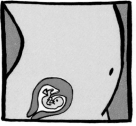

By fourteen weeks it has arms, legs and organs forming its body.

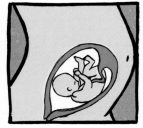

At twenty-four weeks the baby looks like a miniature human being.

At thirty-six weeks the baby is almost ready to be born.

How does a baby get out?

When the time comes, the mother knows that her baby is ready to be born. Her womb is very strong and contains special muscles that are able to push the baby out. When they start to do this it is called 'going into labour'. Her vagina and birth passages loosen up to make room for the baby to get out — through the opening between her legs — but it is usually quite a tight fit!

The baby then starts to live by itself outside its mother for the first time. It cries, breathes, and begins to make little sucking movements with its lips. It can drink milk as soon as it is born.

When a baby is born it is one of the most exciting experiences God gives us.

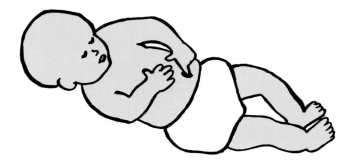

While the baby is in its mother's womb it is not fed on real food. Instead it gets all it needs from its mother's blood. This supply comes to it through a tube going into its tummy button. This tube connects with the cushiony placenta on the inside of its mother's womb. Once a baby has been born, this connection is no longer needed and is cut by the nurse. The placenta slips out of the mother after the birth of the baby.

You were designed to belong

A baby is helpless. It *needs* to belong to a family, or to be cared for by someone. But boys and girls and grown-ups need other people to help them too.

Have you ever been left on your own at home for a little while or had no one to play with in the playground? It's not a nice feeling to be left alone.

God designed people to live in families and to have friends. Belonging to each other is part of how we have been made. God didn't just design your body, he designed you to have feelings and to be able to think about things. He designed you to have a sense of humour.

When God created people he made them so that they could be his friends if they wanted to. He designed you to know him.

Although you can't see God, he is a very special person and you can be friends with him inside yourself. You can belong to God's family made up of people all over the world.

God has designed you so that you are able to love other people. You can love God just as much as you can love your friends and relatives.

Loving is part of being a person — one of the most important parts. This means that you really *do* mind what happens to your friend; you *want* to look after your baby brother; and it makes you feel good when you have done something that makes your dad smile.

It's difficult to explain where feelings, or emotions, come from. Scientists don't know what makes you feel happy or sad, angry, proud, kind, gentle, selfish or unselfish. It all happens in a secret part of your brain that no one understands very much about yet. Scientists don't know exactly what part of your brain lets you feel God or helps you want to be his friend.

We know a lot about the human body and how it works and although scientists understand a lot about the brain, there are still mysteries that no one understands. Scientists know that you are able to love but they don't know exactly where in the brain the loving feelings come from, or how they are made.

One of the most exciting things about being a human is that it means that God created you able to be his friend. God gave you a family and he gave you friends and he wanted you in the world so that you and he could be friends for life.

Keeping you straight — bones

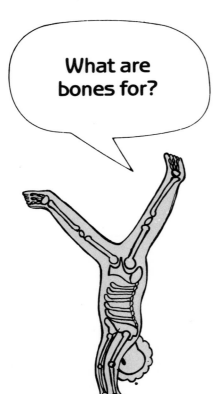

What are bones for?

Your body is made so that you can do lots of things with it. You can hop on one leg, you can carry a heavy load on your head, you can swim, you can stretch up high, and you can lie on the floor and wriggle along if you want to.

Your body is built around a framework of bones, which are joined to one another to make you the shape you are. This framework is called the skeleton.

Your bones do many things. They give your body strength; they hold parts of you rigid so that you are not just a floppy body; and they allow you to stand up straight. Many bones also protect your soft inside.

Some bones hold you in shape — like your backbone. This is made up of small bones joined one on top of the other. They are called vertebrae.

Other bones act as protection for some of the delicate organs in your body and prevent them from getting bruised or squashed. Your brain is so fragile that God gave it a bony covering like the head-piece of a knight in armour —

called the skull. Your lungs and heart are protected by your rib cage.

Bones are very tough and hard. If a surgeon has to cut through someone's thigh bone then he needs to use a strong saw. Your bones are strong because they are full of calcium — a chemical which fills up the spaces between the living bone cells.

Bones that do not have enough calcium bend easily.

How do bones fit together?

You can move your arms round in circles because your shoulder joint is a special sort of joint that allows this kind of movement. Your shoulder joint is called a ball and socket joint, so is your hip joint.

Bones aren't glued together. If they were, you wouldn't be able to move in different directions.

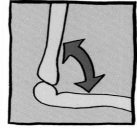

They are joined by three different sorts of joints which allow you to bend and turn in different directions without harming anything.

Your elbow and your knees allow your arms and legs to open and shut. These joints are called hinge joints. They work like a door opening and closing.

All these different joints allow you to do somersaults, handstands, jack-knife dives, backbends and even to walk on your hands. Of course, you also need muscles to move your bones.

You can do a lot with your wrists and ankles and move them in many different ways. This is because the joints there are all slipping joints. They work by rocking slightly.

How does a broken leg mend?

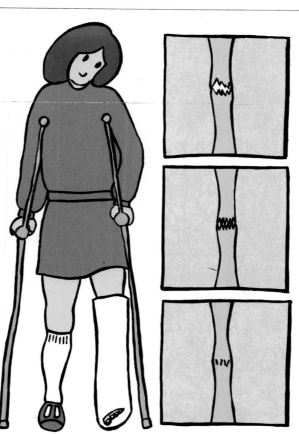

Your body is fairly tough and bends easily. But sometimes if you fall awkwardly you break a bone. A child's broken bone usually mends easily. It's harder if you are an old person.

When a bone breaks, bone cells make strands across the break. These gradually get toughened up by calcium and harden to make a firm mend.

When a doctor puts a plaster cast on a broken bone it is to make sure that the bone mends in the right position. Without the cast it might mend crooked.

Making you move—muscles

Why do we have muscles?

The more you exercise a muscle, the thicker and stronger it gets. Look at athletes — the muscles that are most developed are those that they exercise most.

Bones are no good without muscles — and muscles are no use without bones. It is your muscles that make your bones move.

No one is really made of just 'skin and bones' although a very thin person may be called that. Everybody has muscles covering their bones.

Most muscles join onto bones, and they help you to move different parts of your body.

But you also have a network of tiny muscles that are not attached to bones. When you laugh, little muscles under the skin of your face ripple with enjoyment, your mouth smiles and your eyes crease up and your tongue curls.

How do muscles work?

When you kick, muscles on the front of the top of your leg jerk your knee up and outwards. Then muscles on your foot pull your toes upwards ready for the kick. Other muscles work hard to stop you from falling over while you balance on one leg.

The thinking part of your brain controls most of your muscles.

When you think 'I'm going to miss the bus!' your brain gets your legs to run and makes your arms swing so that you don't topple over.

Most of your muscles come under the direct control of your brain. But there are a few muscles that don't need to wait for orders from the brain but just keep on working. These are special muscles like the heart muscle that goes on pumping as long as you are alive and muscles in your intestines that push food downwards.

The body is made so wonderfully that all your muscle movements are balanced carefully. If you do a cart-wheel then the muscles in your arms, legs, stomach wall and back work in harmony to make the cart-wheel perfect. If you fall over doing it, it is because you have lost your balance and your muscles have stopped working perfectly together.

You can train your muscles and your body to do a perfect cart-wheel if you work hard enough at it.

Waterproof wrapping—skin

What is skin?

Skin is thick in some parts of your body and thin in others. On the soles of your feet is tough skin about 6mm thick to protect the muscles and bones of your feet from pressure. Around your eyes it is very thin — about 0.5mm thick.

Your skin is made up of layers of cells to form a tough outer covering for your body. It keeps germs, water and poisons out and stops your soft insides from getting hurt.

Why do people have different coloured skins?

Are different coloured people the same under their skins?

Everyone's skin contains a brown colouring agent called melanin. This helps to protect your body from damage by the sun's rays.

If you have brown or black skin it is because you have plenty of protective melanin in your skin. This is because you live in a hot country where the sun shines most of the time. Or you may live in a cold country now, but someone way back in your family lived in a hot country. God created you with enough melanin so that you wouldn't be hurt by the sun.

And if you have brown eyes and dark hair then going out in hot sun makes you darker. The melanin in your skin stops you from burning.

But if you have fair hair and blue eyes, you know that going out in hot sun makes your skin go red and burn. That is because you have very little melanin in your skin.

You are exactly the same under your skin as somebody who is a different colour from you. You have the same organs, bones, muscles, blood and brain. All the big things that matter are the same. Smaller things are sometimes different in different races but these are things like how curly your hair is, and other things that don't really matter.

We know that God made all people — and he made us to be different. Different in how we look, and in what we do, and what we are. But he loves us all with the same sort of love.

What is a scar?

If you cut yourself your skin is usually very quick to join up again by itself. If the cut is very deep then it may need stitching up to hold the cut bits together. A good strong join is made by the body — this is called a scar. It often isn't pretty but it won't come undone, which is what matters most!

Sweat gland   Nerve   Hair

There are sweat glands in your skin. They pour out sweat when you are hot and your sweat evaporates to keep you cool.

Tiny nerves run in your skin and let you feel things. Some people have hairs in their skin as well.

Bits and pieces—teeth, hair and nails

How many teeth
have I got?
What are they for?

Can you imagine what it would be like if you didn't have any teeth? You'd look funny, but worse than that, you wouldn't be able to chew your food and break it down ready to be digested. You'd only be able to drink.

When babies are born they don't need teeth because they suck milk. But after a few months a baby starts to teethe, and its baby teeth or 'milk' teeth come through. These milk teeth are small to fit a baby's small mouth. But as you grow, your adult teeth grow up and push the milk teeth out.

Adults have 28 teeth plus an extra four called 'wisdom' teeth. You are supposed to be wise by the time your wisdom teeth come through in your teens or later — but some people's wisdom teeth never come through!

Your teeth are designed for the jobs they do. The front ones — called incisors — are teeth perfect for cutting. Next to them are your canines which are excellent for gripping and tearing. At the side and back are pre-molars and molars designed for grinding food.

Your tooth aches when something is wrong in its centre and the nerve sends a message to the brain which makes you feel pain. This tells you something needs putting right and you go to your dentist.

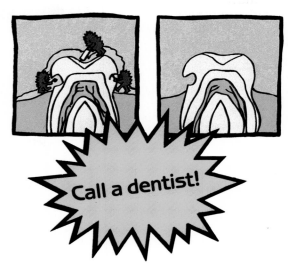

Call a dentist!

All teeth are covered by an outer protective coat of enamel. Under this is dentine which is hard and makes up most of the tooth. In the centre is the pulp, containing nerves and blood vessels. Nearly two-thirds of each tooth is embedded in the jaw.

If you don't look after your teeth properly, dental decay breaks through the outer covering and causes trouble.

It is important to look after your teeth and avoid dental decay by brushing them often, and avoiding sweet, sugary foods between meals. It is also important to visit your dentist regularly.

Are all babies born with hair?

Everyone has hair on their heads unless they are ill or old.

Some babies are born bald and others with thick hair on their heads. If you are born with lots of hair, it usually all falls out and you get a fresh crop of hair which is the colour your hair will be for life. A bald baby soon grows hair too.

The colour of your hair is something you inherit from your parents. That's why members of the same family often have the same colour hair as each other.

Each hair on your head stays there between two to six years. Your hair often grows at a rate of about 15cm each year.

What are nails for?

Nails, on the ends of your toes and fingers, stop these ends from getting frayed or hurt.

Nails are made of skin which has turned horny. They grow up under the skin from just above your last toe or finger joint. Nails grow at the rate of around 6mm every month. If you have been ill then it shows on your finger nails by a little white part.

Your body's telephone—nerves

What are nerves?
Why do we
have them?

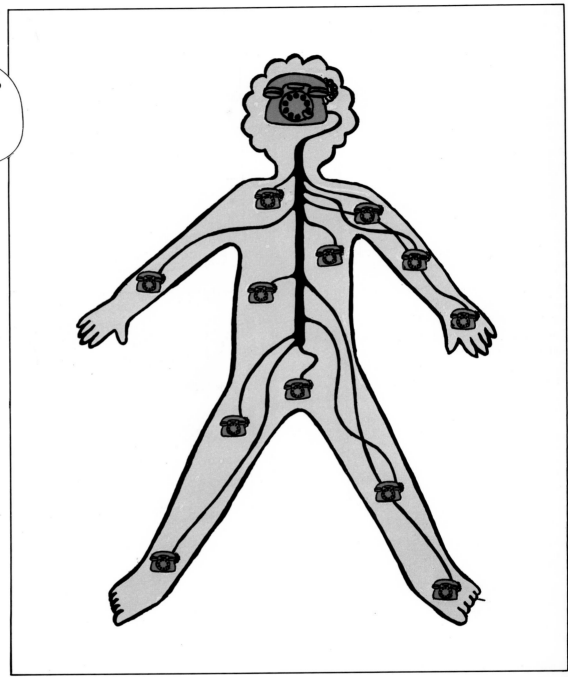

All over your body is a
network of nerves,
carrying messages
backwards and
forwards all the time.

Nerves act like a telephone network, telling your brain what it needs to know at high speed.

It is vital to have this fast communications service both to keep your body doing all the ordinary things it does like walking, eating and playing and also to stop you getting hurt.

Your spinal cord is a bit like the trunk of a tree. This runs from the bottom of your back up to your brain carrying messages from all the different nerves in each part of your body. Your backbone protects the soft spinal cord. Messages are also passed downwards from the brain to different parts of your body through the spinal cord and then through big nerves and down to the tiniest nerves. These messages are carried incredibly fast.

Your brain can sometimes over-ride automatic responses, if you want it to. Your finger usually moves away from intense heat. But you *can* tell your finger to stay in a candle flame — if you want to do this, and risk getting burnt!

At other times you cannot over-ride automatic actions. If you breathe a peanut into your wind-pipe then it is impossible for you to stop coughing until the peanut is coughed out or settled in the bottom of your lungs where it would cause silent trouble.

If you touch something really hot, your hand is automatically drawn away from the heat. You do this without thinking because your brain tells different muscles to get moving and get you out of danger.

There are tiny nerve cells under your skin and in other parts of your body. Different nerve cells do different things — they can feel the shape of things, or feel temperature, or pain. These nerve cells are linked up to tiny branch nerves which run to join big nerves, like small twigs on a tree joining larger twigs and then branches and then the tree trunk.

What happens if you break your neck?

Your body is tough and flexible in many ways, but it is also easily hurt. In many cases the body can heal itself from hurt — but sometimes an injury is very serious. You might break your neck by diving into shallow water without putting out your arms and hitting your head on the bottom, for example, or by being in a road accident when your head suddenly jerks backwards.

This can damage your spinal cord.

Sometimes it only bruises the cord; other times it might break it altogether. This means that the messages that usually tell the body what to do cannot get through. Some parts, or all, of the body cannot move. This is called being paralysed.

Every part of your nervous system is usually working perfectly in harmony. It is so good, you never really think about it. God is a good designer.

Secrets of your senses

What are the five senses?

You have five different ways of knowing about things through your five senses — touch, taste, sight, sound and smell. They are linked up to your

1

2

3

4

5

brain through your nerves and quickly tell your brain what is happening. You are not even aware of anything happening as it's so fast.

Your five senses work together. If one sense stops, others work harder. If you are blind, you know what is happening through touch, smell, taste and hearing — and you can hear much better than other people as your sense of hearing works overtime to make up for your loss of sight.

What's that smell?

You use your nose to smell things and a nerve sends a message to your brain explaining what the smell is like.

Why do sweet and sour taste different?

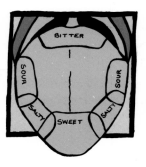

BITTER
SOUR
SOUR
SALTY
SALTY
SWEET

You taste through one of the thousands of tiny taste buds on your tongue.

Taste buds can pick out the difference between sweet, sour, salt and bitter.

Different areas of your tongue are sensitive to each of these four flavours.

What do your finger-tips tell you?

Your fingers, and other parts of your body that are used for feeling, are thick with nerve cells specially designed for feeling things. These nerve cells join to other nerves which tell your brain what you are touching — whether it's rough or smooth, hot or cold, wet or dry, and so on.

What's that sound?

The part of your ear that you can see only helps to collect sound but it isn't the most important part of your ear. The bits which have nerve cells are hidden away inside. The way you are able to recognize so many different sounds is fantastic.

When you hear a sound, messages are sent to the brain. It is your brain that tells you whether your mum is calling that dinner's ready, or a band is playing, or a car is chugging down the road.

A tube runs inwards from your ear and carries sound waves down it which strike the ear drum. This makes the membrane between your middle and inner ear vibrate. The fluid in the inner ear beats time and brushes against the nerve cells which send messages to the brain. The brain knows what the sound is.

What can you see?

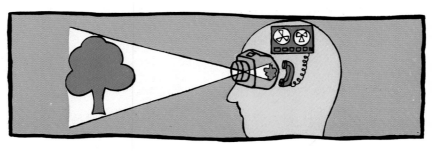

When you look at something, your eye can tell you all kinds of things at the same time. It is able to tell whether the thing you are looking at is dark or light, what shape it is, what colour it is, and what happens when it moves.

As you look, you can immediately tell whether the thing is a tree, your teacher, a clown, a house, an elephant, or waves on the sea.

Rays of light travel through a lens near the front of your eye and are focussed on the back of your eye on the retina. This is full of nerve cells that pass messages back through nerves to your brain, so that you know what it is you are looking at.

Your five senses let you know what is happening around you. If it is something bad, you may feel frightened or sad. If it is something good, you feel happy. Seeing the sun shine in the summer, smelling the salty sea breeze, feeling the wind tousle your hair, licking your favourite ice-cream, and stroking your pet gives you a warm, happy feeling — it's a wonderful day you'll remember all your life. Without all five of your senses you'd miss having every part of this rich memory.

More amazing than any computer—the brain

What does my brain do?

We often say that someone is 'brainy' because they are good at school work. But we are all 'brainy' because everybody has a brain!

Without a brain you wouldn't be able to do anything. Your brain makes you able to think; it helps you to learn, and to remember; and it makes sure that all the different parts of you work together.

Your brain is inside your head, in your skull, which protects it from getting hurt.

It looks like a big walnut — in two halves that are grey and craggy.

If you look at a human brain, you'd never believe all the wonderful things it does — it doesn't look very impressive. But your brain is better than the best microcomputer ever invented. It is more intricate, works faster and is more clever. No computer has as many functions as the human brain.

We use our memory to help us learn things. And we also use our memories to remember things that happen to us — good things and bad things.

How does it work?

A gymnast's brain makes sure that every part of her body works perfectly together.

Every year scientists find out more about how the human brain works, but they still don't know everything about it.

Information is fed to the brain by nerves from all the different parts of your body. Then instructions are sent to the body down the same nerves.

Special parts of your brain receive the information that is fed to it by your five senses. Your brain can store this information away, so that you remember what was recorded in the brain and can use it in the future.

Your brain does lots of other important things too. It controls what is happening inside you. It controls your body's heating system, making sure it stays at a good level, and it also controls the amount of fluid in your blood so that you have exactly the quantity that is best for you.

Exciting things happen in your brain. You may decide, 'I want to be good at gym!' You think that in your brain. Then somewhere inside your brain, your will — the something inside you which decides you want to do something and makes you do it — encourages you to start practising. Your brain helps you remember how to balance, and then makes each muscle work with the others so that you move easily. Your brain helps you to train your muscles and to learn by practising how to control your body and make it do what you want it to do.

Your brain is so complex that it makes you realize how powerful God must be to have created something so wonderful that doesn't break down.

Who made me?

How did I get here?

If you ask different people how human beings got into the world then you may get some different answers.

Some people will tell you that you have descended from animals, but that you have developed more than the most well-developed and clever animal.

Others believe that after God finished creating the world and the animals, he did something even more special — he made people.

People are different from animals in more than appearance. You can think things out for yourself, do maths, write stories, paint pictures, enjoy sports and play. You are also able to love your friends and family in a different way from the way animals love. Above all, you are able to be a friend of God — you can talk to him and sometimes you can feel him close to you. Animals can't do this.

Why do we die?

In the beginning, when God made people, there was no such thing as death and dying. The whole of creation was good.

But the people God had made ignored his instructions and disobeyed him (this is called 'sin') and from then onwards death came into the world. You can read about this in the Bible, in the book of Genesis.

God did not want people to die, and the Bible tells us that God's son, Jesus Christ, came into the world to save us from sin, and give us a new life, which goes on even after our bodies have died.

As you get older your body gradually begins to wear out, so that finally you die. Your heart stops beating, your brain stops sending messages out and your tired body stops working. Your body will be buried or cremated.

But something wonderful happens to the real important 'you' that isn't part of your body. The real 'you' stays alive and goes to be with God. The real you doesn't float around, nor is it stored away to come back as another person at another time. But the Bible says that anyone who loves God and believes in Jesus Christ goes on to be with him after they die. Dying is not the end of the story.

What is life for?

Did you know that God knows exactly how many hairs you have on your head? Jesus tells us that God loves us and knows so much about us that he even knows how many hairs we have.

Living is the most important thing you are doing now.

Your life can be a wonderful and exciting adventure. Anyone's life can be exciting. But the most marvellous way to live is to live as a friend of God's.

Because God made you, and because he is the maker of the whole of creation, he cares for you and he wants to show us how to live.

We have the Bible as the 'maker's instructions' for our life; and we have our families, and God's family too, to look after us and show us how to live.

The Bible tells us lots of wonderful things about God and us. It says that even before you were born, while you were still inside your mother, God knew everything about you. It also says that God wants you to be his friend and to know him and love him too, for ever.

Index